INVESTING IN
FOREIGN PROPERTY
THE BEST TIPS AND PRACTICAL ADVICE
FOR BUYING FOREIGN PROPERTY AND
LIVING ABROAD SAFELY

STEFANO LUCATELLO

PUBLISHED BY:
SPARKLE DESIGN & PRINT
I-KAN BUSINESS CENTRE
BEDFORD
UNITED KINGDOM

Disclaimer

This book will provide you with authoritative, accurate information and advice. Please remember that it's a quick and practical walk through this huge topic.

It's meant to give you pointers, tips and practical warnings.

I have endeavoured to ensure that all the information contained is up to date and accurate.

Many markets move quickly as do the laws and regulations governing the purchase of foreign property.

Before buying you MUST take professional investment, financial and legal advice.

If you decide to buy, email me at: stefanol@kobaltlaw.co.uk or call me at Kobalt Law LLP, +44 207 739 1700

We would then give you detailed legal advice on your potential investment.

Neither I nor my firm, Kobalt Law LLP, can be held responsible for any losses, financial or other hardship, if things don't go according to plan, even if you have read this guide.

Contents

Stefano Lucatello

Foreword

Irrespective of whether you are just thinking about buying a foreign property or you have already started the long and arduous journey, this is the book for you.

Investing in Foreign Property...the Ultimate Guide to Investing Safely is practical, hard hitting and to the point.

Investing in Foreign Property...the Ultimate Guide to Investing Safely is filled with practical tips, comments, experiences and observations; it is guaranteed to keep you safe whilst you pick your dream property abroad.

Investing in Foreign Property...the Ultimate Guide to Investing Safely is full of general and more specific information and guidance. It is not meant to be the longest book in the world, but a practical, to the point guide.

Keep a copy of *Investing in Foreign Property...the Ultimate Guide to Investing Safely* with you at all times, both before you book the first inspection trip and, more importantly, whilst you are there searching for the property you imagine yourself sitting in, drinking that cold refreshing glass of prosecco or champagne.

Investing in Foreign Property...the Ultimate Guide to Investing Safely covers the most important, life-saving tips, whether you are still to buy, you have bought or you are thinking of leaving the United Kingdom, for a full lifestyle change, to live and work or

just relax and retire for the last years of your life.
Investing in Foreign Property...the Ultimate Guide to Investing Safely
is a comprehensive handbook covering everyday topics, and
represents an up to date source of general information.

Investing in Foreign Property...the Ultimate Guide to Investing Safely
will help you save money, time, and lots of grief, and will repay
your investment, many times over!

Happy hunting!

Raymond Aaron
New York Times Best-selling Author

Acknowledgements

My sincere thanks to my "Carissima Mamma Maria", who, when I was 11, told me I would become an international lawyer!

To my "journalist" trained father, Luigi, who taught me many of the book writing skills, necessary to write this book.

To my partner Marilyn, who took the time to read the draft versions of this book and who guides my law practice through everyday life.

A special thanks to my team of highly skilled international lawyers, who work with me at Kobalt Law LLP and who form an integral part of the international property law guidance and services, which Kobalt Law LLP provides to the general public.

Finally, I want to extend my sincere thanks to You, the reader of my first book.

It's a great privilege to impart what I have learnt, as an international property lawyer, in the last 25 years, which hopefully keeps you safe!

Stefano Lucatello

Chapter 1
In the Beginning...

This book comes with a personal health warning...!

Unless you follow my tips, buying a property abroad may damage your health and may lead to death...!!

Buying property abroad is no less difficult than buying a property in the UK. The road to buying a foreign property is fraught with the same dangers and pitfalls that you find when buying a property in the UK.

Get it wrong and you could lose your health, sanity and the property. It could be demolished, without any redress.

This handy practical guide is meant as a reference tool, for you to take abroad and consult whilst on your journey of discovery. It covers the main points you need to be aware of at each stage.

Follow my tips and advice and you won't go far wrong.

This practical guide will see you buy the property of your dreams and not turn what should be the road to paradise into the nightmare of a lifetime and a living hell.

My Starting Point

So tell me this...why, when buying abroad, do 95% of potential buyers not engage the services of an English specialist foreign property lawyer, to guide them through the maze of intricacies

and pitfalls that are there waiting to trip them up?
The majority of potential buyers go with the agent's "advice" and use a local lawyer, recommended to them, not having checked them out and not having done even a basic due diligence exercise, which you would carry out when instructing an English Solicitor .

The majority of you reading this all own your own home. So did you buy it without a Solicitor or one of the other conveyancing professions in the UK? Of course not!

Not even I, who am a conveyancing Solicitor, would buy my own home using my own skills as a lawyer! You always instruct a lawyer, because they are paid to spot things you would not, and they consider matters that would never enter your head as ever being a worthwhile consideration.

Why, when you don't understand the language and the different system of law, do the majority of potential buyers just rely on the foreign agent, who has no interest whatsoever in protecting the buyer, but is there to sell the property and account only to the vendor?

I decided to write this guide to help potential buyers like you, after having specialised for over 20 years in assisting foreign property buyers to invest safely, and having experienced the majority of the possible tricks of the trade, pitfalls and problems facing potential buyers, like you.

When I used to practice as a foreign property Solicitor in Yorkshire, I used to receive calls on Monday mornings, during the summer season, about 11.50am, just after the Alicante flight had landed at Humberside airport.

The call would go along the lines of..." Hello, I saw your law firm's advert at Humberside airport and I've just landed from Alicante, where ......" at which point I would interject and finish the sentence by saying..." you and your wife signed a reservation agreement for a villa and paid a reservation fee, without reading the contract and you've decided you don't want it and now want to pull out..?."

The caller would then say..." Wow, how did you know that?" I would say..." because I have calls like yours every week on a Monday, during the summer season, when at least one couple like you rings me for help!"

The moral of this story is this.....do not leave your brains in the car at the UK airport carpark, only to pick them up, when you return.....!!!!!!!!!!!

Why Buy a Property Abroad?

One evening some friends come round and during the conversation they tell you that they recently bought a property in Spain and that they would like you to come and stay with them. They tell you that it went really well, because they followed my tips and guidance and that it was so easy.!.

 That evening you and your wife decide that, because the money sat in your "interest bearing" account, but isn't bearing as much interest as it used to, perhaps it would do better in another form of investment, and you agree to embark on a journey of discovery, like your friends.

Stop!....think!....take a deep breath... Collect your thoughts...

There are four primary reasons for investing in property abroad.
The Four Main Reasons

Firstly, to use it as a true investment: one which you do not occupy for your own purposes during the holidays. The property has been bought with the money that was in your less than "interest bearing" account and so you want to derive a greater return than before. Remember that capital growth and rental yields can increase as well as decrease.

Secondly, you might just want to buy it for holidays, as a second home, so that you, your family and friends can enjoy it three times a year.

Ask yourself this....are you happy to go to the same place every year?

Thirdly, you might want to have it as part leisure and part investment. How do you go about renting it out? What rules apply?

Fourthly, you might have retired and decided to spend the last part of your lives in a hotter, more pleasant climate and experience a total lifestyle change.

Consider whether you will have to work once you move. Can you pursue your job or profession in that country? Will that country's authorities recognise the qualifications you have been awarded in the UK?

Each one of these four scenarios brings with it different considerations and problems. Get the answers right and you will have made the best investment of your life....... Get them wrong and you could have lost all your money, your home in the UK and in some cases, your health!

The one word which links and underpins all four choices available, whichever it may be, is the word "location".

So remember... "location, location, location"

Which Country & Factors to Consider?

Consider the following factors and choices:

Off-plan or existing property?
Inland or coastal?
Isolated or noisy?
Apartment, town house or villa?
Freehold/leasehold/timeshare/fractional/leaseback?
Garden or no garden?
Close to a town centre or on the outskirts?
Close to public transport or walking distance to the shops?
How close to the nearest airport?
Close to the beach?
Close to local health and social services?
Pets or no pets?
Can I learn the language easily and integrate?
Will you miss your friends and family?

The Main Markets

As a first time investor I would advise choosing one of the "established primary foreign markets". Those are Spain, France, Italy and Portugal.

They are all within 2 hours' flight journey from the main UK airports.

They are the markets that the English traditionally go for, and the climates are appealing. The cost of living in those countries is cheaper than the UK and they all offer a variety of attractions, whereas the UK does not.

These are the countries which are the safest and which have the lowest "risk to reward" returns.

We then have the "secondary investment markets".
These are those countries which emerged in the early 2000's; countries such as the USA, Bulgaria, Dubai, Cape Verde, Dominican Republic, Brazil, Argentina, Central Latin American States, Isla Margarita, The West Indies, Egypt, Tunisia, Morocco, Mexico and Southeast Asia.

The "tertiary investment markets" are those such as Ghana, Nigeria, Mozambique, the Philippines, and Angola.

Here the 'risk to reward" ratio is seen as higher, with the distance to these locations, being one of the most important factors, as well as the countries' unstable governments and economies.

These countries are famous for the major scams that have emerged over the years; false promises, land that doesn't exist, no real developers, websites that are only "smoke and mirrors", alternative investments, such as oil producing crops, other types of "futures" and the like.

Chapter 2
Finding the Property of your Dreams

It's quite often the case that you are bored on holiday and you resort to looking through estate agents' windows. Many well-known English estate agents have offices abroad. Names such as Knight Frank, Hamptons International, Chestertons and Savills.

It's my view that you are not in the correct state of mind, whilst on holiday, to make such important decisions and you may fall foul to agents that target the UK visitor.

You should delay such decisions to a correctly planned identification visit, which has, as its only scope, the purpose of identifying the location and the property.

It does make sense to choose a country you like and you know. Explore the best areas and regions, where you feel that you won't lose interest later.

Always visit many agents in the area of choice.

Take your Time

Never choose the first property you see. You may be shown "not so good" properties and then a much "higher spec" property which draws you in. Beware of this tactic.

See the property in different types of light and at different times of the year.

Never sign any form of paper whilst at the agent's. Never commit to anything. Come home and consider the proposition in the cold light of day.

If you buy from a UK based agent, they're subject to rules on selling, especially regarding misrepresentation as to words used and computer generated images. Agents who misrepresent with words or images could be open to legal action under the Misrepresentation Act.

UK agents who sell online are also subject to the "distance selling regulations", which came into effect in 2014.

Check whether the agent is a member of AIPP (the Association of International Property Professionals).

This is a trade organisation based in London, which carries out due diligence on its members so as to give the public a greater degree of security, when buying from the agent or a developer.

The logo can only be displayed by a recognised member, who has been vetted beforehand.

If that member acts unprofessionally or illegally, then AIPP can sanction that member and take disciplinary action.

How Developers Sell "Off Plan" Property

Some examples are:
In newspapers
In luxury magazines

By direct cold calling
Online adverts
SMS campaigns
Email campaigns
At international property shows
At educational and investment training courses.

Avoid Inspection Trips

You may be tempted to visit a "yet to be built development", or a built development, by paying £99, for a 3 day "inspection trip".

Beware...it's not a holiday... You may well be harassed, threatened, bullied, coerced and possibly forced into a decision, which may not be in your best interests. Now, this is very extreme and most agents are great, but beware, all the same... The trip is usually arranged for the developer to get you on your own and to badger you until he gets what he wants from you... a signature that commits you to buy from him.

Believe me; I've heard of all kinds of tricks being used and stunts being pulled by developers, even so far as locking the buyer in a room, until he put his signature on the dotted line!

It's true to say that not all agents are like this.....! So if you want certainty,... use AIPP registered agents.

Never use an inspection trip, unless it's from a reputable agent... Get there yourself and make your own accommodation arrangements. Never buy on the basis that "they're selling like hot cakes".

Take my advice; there will always be another better proposition round the corner, if you miss the first one.

Buying "off plan" used to be seen as a way to a "quick profit"....it's not always the case nowadays. Many people have invested unwisely, only to find that the developer has either not finished the project or gone into liquidation. Always ask for the deposit to be refundable and for there to be a cooling off period.

Check with the AIPP and other groups, if the developer has a proven track record and read internet forums as well as online comments or articles; carry out online company searches as to financial stability and look at the company's accounts

Developer Bank Guarantees

Check whether he will give a guarantee to protect your investment. Get a proper payment plan from the developer.

In many European countries, developers must give bank guarantees and in some, such as Morocco, they cannot take monies from buyers unless they have built the foundations with their own money first.

In Italy, bank guarantees must be renewed every 12 months.

Never buy a property unseen or without visiting it, irrespective of how cheap it sounds or how good value; never buy in a country you have never visited.

Ensure the developer is also the owner of the land to be developed.

Sometimes developers enter into side agreements with the real beneficial owners of the land. You must know who you are contracting with, in case something goes wrong.

You may end up having to enter into two contracts to secure your position; one with the developer to build your home and one with the owner of the land. This will ensure he will actually convey the land to the developer or you when the time comes; otherwise, you might end up with a home, but no right to access it!

Get someone to monitor the progress of the build. Get regular FOTO updates... Not words...

Always study the geography and the meteorological conditions and natural hazards, such as high water levels, hurricanes, volcanoes, and earthquakes.

Other Sources of Property

Another way of buying is from the owner, by way of private treaty.

Beware...no less due diligence is necessary when buying from an owner.

Auctions provide cheap and usually repossessed property, especially foreign based auctions.

Auctions are governed by particular rules. It pays to learn them well first! Usually a property pack is available for inspection some days before the auction takes place.

This will contain title and search papers, a plan and other particular information, such as an energy certificate, as is required throughout the EU.

More and more property has been sold in the last 10 years at educational or training courses, where new and budding property investors are taught how to create their property investment portfolios.

At the end they are offered something "special", a "pre-release to the public" offer, which no one else has access to........!

Never buy at such a training or educational session. Treat them for what they are...nothing more ....nothing less.

Go home and then consider your options .The urge to buy, whilst the adrenaline is pumping must be resisted; you will regret signing the next day.

Property shows, such as "A Place in the Sun Live", which is a spin-off of the successful channel 4 TV programme and other such property buying shows, have proved successful venues for agents wanting to sell property.

Again, listen, learn, look and don't sign.

Come to see me at the Kobalt Law LLP stand and I will give you impartial guidance!

Why not come onto the Kobalt Law LLP stand and listen to the free seminars which deal with my top tips to follow, when considering buying property abroad?

Chapter 3
Financing the Purchase

Consider how much you have to spend and how you will finance the purchase, before you start looking.

Budget for the entire "one off" purchase costs before you start.

Create a "costs list". It should include, amongst other things:

Purchase price
Stamp duty/ land tax
Community charges
Registration fee
Vat (on new builds only)
Survey fees
Search fees
Legal fees (English specialist lawyer)
Foreign notary fees and vat
Insurance
Mortgage brokerage fees
Money exchange commission

Using your Own Capital

Buying your property with your own savings is by far the best and cheapest way. It means you owe no one or no bank any money, but it does mean that, unless you are exceptionally rich, it might leave you short, if you need the money quickly, for some unforeseen eventuality.

On the other hand, why use your own money if you can use someone else's and repay them over a long period?

It may be the case that you are leaving the UK permanently and that you will use all or part of your UK net sale proceeds to buy the property.

General Borrowing Tips

If you decide to borrow, always use an independent broker registered with the FCA.

If you can't do this completely, you can borrow part of the funds.

Borrowing on your UK property to invest abroad is one choice.

Make sure you can afford the repayments and that you are not reliant on rental income to meet your repayments.

Ensure you can meet the repayments if the interest rates increase, your property can't be rented or the tenant doesn't pay you.

My advice is not to use your own house as collateral on a foreign property investment.

In certain countries, you can take on the mortgage that your seller obtained and continue paying it, as if it had been granted to you, until the end of the term.

Borrowing from a Foreign Bank

Specialist UK-based foreign mortgage brokers exist and they can assist you. Check their credentials as always.

If you borrow from a foreign bank, you will secure the debt on your foreign property. The likelihood is that the loan will be in a foreign currency.

The lender will require a survey and valuation to be carried out before it will approve the loan.

Ensure you understand the terms of the mortgage and the fact that exchange rates may play a big part in your ability to repay the mortgage. Don't overstretch yourself.

If you are paid in sterling, you should repay the loan in sterling and not euros, Swiss francs or dollars.

The Main Kinds of Mortgages

Interest and repayment
Interest only
Tracker mortgage
Fixed rate
Variable rate

Other Types of Funding

Using your SIPP
Joint venture with another person(s)
Crowd funding
Vulture funding

Rent to buy (commonly known as vendor's finance)
If you are leaving the UK permanently and you can afford it, rent your home in the UK out, just in case you have to return quickly, following a medical condition or death in the family.

Chapter 4
Legal Advice and Assistance

Overseas laws and regulations are totally different from our own common law system. If you buy in Europe, the system of law is called the "civil law code".

I have appeared on many TV programmes and recounted many horrendous stories of buyers losing all their money, because they didn't follow the simple rules, set out in this book.

I cannot stress how important it is for prospective buyers to seek independent dispassionate legal advice. The same goes for independent financial and valuation advice.

The lawyer must not have any connection with the agent or the developer.

The lawyer should speak both languages fluently and be qualified in that country's laws.

At Kobalt Law LLP, we have a team of foreign qualified lawyers, based in our London office, who meet all those criteria.

In foreign countries, the lawyer does not deal with the house buying process. This is dealt with by a government appointed representative called a "notary".

Beware; the word "notary" has nothing to do with our English "notary public".

The "notary" is an independent state appointed representative, who checks that the vendor is the legitimate seller and the buyer is who he says he is.

He then checks that the legal title to the property is correct and that the parties have the correct contractual paperwork, that the full purchase price is declared on the transfer deed.

Finally he checks that the vendor does not owe any local, regional or national taxes, before releasing the balance of the net sale proceeds he has retained, as a government security or bond.

This is then released some 3 to 6 months later, dependent on the country of purchase.

Remember: having a notary is not enough, as he does not represent either the vendor or the purchaser.

Beware of any seller who wants you to under declare the full purchase price. This is illegal in most countries and is known as " ante-money laundering". This is an imprisonable offence in the UK and most other countries.

The Legal Process

Initially, the lawyer will engage with the agent or the developer or with the vendor direct.

He will ask all the questions and make all the enquiries required, so that you know the whole story.

He will carry out searches and check who the owners are, and if there are any debts, financial or other charges and easements (such as rights of pedestrian, vehicular or animal passage, especially in the countryside) registered on the property, which will need to be paid off or highlighted before or on completion.

He will check whether the property has a "habitation licence", which allows you to connect to the utilities. Without this you cannot connect and you will have a bought a worthless asset.

Remember: if the property is in the countryside, check if there are any rights of way across your land or rights to use the land in a particular way, which your purchase is subject to (ancient or recently created rights to cut and take crops, such as wheat, olives, fruits etc, or persons who, in any other way, have prior rights over parts of your land).

In Spain, especially in the Valencia region, if you buy in the countryside, check that your house was granted the correct planning and regulatory permissions when it was originally built. If not you could well find your house being demolished by the local authority, without great financial redress.

Remember all those nightmare stories of the "Valencia" region of Spain?

It's true to say that a new criminal law came into effect on 1st July 2015, which forces the builder to hand over all the illegal profits, which resulted from the illegal bulldozing of a person's home. A further piece of administrative law comes into effect on 1st October 2015, which compensates a person, who loses a property, legitimately, to a local planning demolition order.

Your lawyer will then ensure the preliminary purchase contract is correctly drafted and well-balanced, incorporating any conditions and special clauses particular to your purchase.

He will make the initial written offer for you, in such as way so as not to bind you.

Once the offer is accepted, the contract, called a "preliminary contract", will be signed and a deposit (usually 10%), is paid across.

This is similar to and the equivalent of the English process known as "exchanging contracts".

Beware: there are different types of contract, which give the respective parties different rights, obligations and advantages. Check these out before signing.

For example, in France, after signing the contract, there is then a "cooling off period" of 10 days for the purchaser to think about his intended purchase. He is therefore given time to pull out, if he has second thoughts.

The 10 day period starts from the day after the contract, signed by both parties, arrives back, by recorded delivery, to the UK address of the buyer.

The purchaser can get out of it, by giving written notice to the seller, before the seventh day and with the full repayment of his deposit.

Fixtures and Fittings

It is usual, when buying a property abroad, to also include most, if not all, of the contents in the house and garden (except for personal items).

This gives rise to three considerations:

Firstly: attach a list of all the fixtures and fittings included in the sale, so that the list forms part of the contract. In this way, it is legally binding and if the vendor takes the items away, you can sue him.

Secondly: there will be some form of value attributed to the fixtures and fittings, which in most countries reduces the stamp duty or land tax duty payable at the moment the purchase is completed.

Thirdly: if the sum attributed to the fixtures and fittings is over-inflated, the local tax man has the right to reopen the purchase contract and say that the valuation attributed is too high. He can then charge you more tax, over and above what you have paid, and perhaps also interest and a penalty.

Having a Survey Carried Out

Before you sign the contract have a survey carried out. Make sure it's a structural survey. This will cost about €1000 including VAT.

It's well worth it, as you will only waste the survey fees as opposed to losing all your hard earned money, when it's too late to pull out, as you have "exchanged contracts"!

Sellers and agents in foreign countries do not like the English habit of carrying out surveys, as it slows the process down. Ignore this and do what you would do in the UK. Have one carried out.

Each country has qualified registered experts, (in France called an "expert geometre" and in Italy called "geometra"), that you can find online.

Get one who is local to your proposed property purchase, as he will be familiar with local problems, such as land geology, earthquakes, landslip, mining, abnormal substances in the land, salt erosion and any other local rules and regulations that may apply.

In France, a vendor cannot go to contract unless he has provided the buyer with a full survey which includes a section on the presence or otherwise of termites (more prevalent, the further south you buy), asbestos and lead. If any of these are found, then the sale cannot proceed until the relevant problem has been eliminated.

Can Foreign Persons Buy?

Check that the country you are buying in allows foreigners to buy and, if not, how you can safely and legally buy.

In France, all sales are subject to the local authority's (known as "comune" or "mairie") "droit de preemption", or "right of first refusal".

This means that, once both parties have signed the preliminary contract, this is sent back to the chosen "notaire"; he will then register the interest in sale and notify the local authority of the vendor's intention to sell.

The local authority then has anything between one and three months to reply, as to whether it will allow the sale to go ahead or whether it will exercise its option and buy the property at the same contract price.

This is historical and is used to protect land or buildings of particular interest, such as land with an "archaeological" interest.

Until written permission is issued by the "comune" to the notaire, the sale is not deemed contractually binding.

As a rule, in Turkey, all foreigners need to get military permission and in Croatia and Tunisia, permission must be sought from the governor and the government respectively.

Countries such as Thailand don't allow a "non Thai citizen" to buy in his own name.

This means you have to incorporate a Thai company and choose a local person, as a controlling/majority shareholder (usually 51%).

This is not good if you have never met that person.

Even if you do know that person, always a have a "declaration of trust" drafted by a lawyer and signed by the local Thai citizen, in which he acknowledges that, although he holds the majority of the shares, you are still the beneficial owner. It also confirms he can't mortgage, sell or in any other way charge the land or the property you have invested in, without your written permission.

Fiscal Codes & Tax Numbers

Most foreign countries require a non-resident purchaser to obtain some form of a "tax or fiscal code number". Similar to our tax number, it allows the national tax authority to keep you on its radar. You cannot complete a transaction without such a code. It must appear in the final sale deed.

Dealing with Developers in "Off Plan" Purchases

When buying a "new build", ensure the builder has obtained the habitation certificate and permission for first occupancy, as well as all other planning and building regulations consents.
Ensure that the land and the building itself have been registered on one title deed and not separate deeds, and that there are no hidden charges or mortgages.

Developer Guarantees

When you buy a new property, usually the builder must give you a 10 year guarantee for serious defects and a 2 year guarantee for minor defects.

If buying a new build ensure it has all the permissions to connect into water, gas, electricity, sewerage and other public connections like telephones and maybe internet.

After the preliminary contracts have been signed by both parties and the deposit is paid, there is little to do but wait and arrange the completion date; this depends on the local notary's availability.

The "Completion Ceremony"

Once the notary has chosen a suitable date for you to attend, the completion meeting or "ceremony" will then occur at the notary's office. You will have to attend in person on the day of completion.

If you can't attend in person, you will have to prepare a power of attorney.
The power of attorney appoints a person you trust, or one of the

notary's employees or assistants, to attend in your place and sign the papers on completion.

If you have a power of attorney prepared in the UK, ensure it is in English and the foreign language of the country you are buying in.

The power will have to be signed in front of an English notary public, who must legalize your signature, by looking at your current passport and checking that the details in that match all the details on the power of attorney.

Once he has done that he will place his stamp, signature and red seal on the power, and sew it together with green tape.

The power must be sent to the UK Government, at the Foreign and Commonwealth office (FCO) at Admiralty Arch in London or at the regional office in Milton Keynes, where the notary public's signature is checked against the list of practising notary publics in the UK, to verify its authenticity.

The FCO will place its confirmation, by way of a certificate called an "apostille" or certificate (depending on whether the country you are buying in is a signatory to the 1961 Hague Convention), which then confers the validity and necessary recognition to the power of attorney, that the foreign notary or government requires. This then allows the donee of the power to act in accordance with the contents of the power.

At the completion meeting, the notary will go through the final completion transfer deed, which he will have prepared and submitted, in draft format, to the parties for approval, some days before the ceremony, together with all the plans and drawings, which must all be signed by the parties and the notary.

Please note that unless you speak that particular language fluently, the notary is forbidden to continue. You will therefore have to appoint and pay for an independent translator or interpreter, who will translate the proceedings and papers for you, as the notary goes through them.
This usually costs another 300 Euros.

The notary then goes through the preliminary contract and reviews the pre-completion searches, which he or one of his assistants had carried out again, a day earlier, to ensure that nothing has changed on the land, such as a registration of a new mortgage or charge, or a sale to another person had been attempted.

If there is a mortgage to sign, he will also read through this and ensure you understand its contents clearly, which are also explained in the final deed. There will usually be someone appointed to attend from the bank to sign the mortgage deed in front of the notary.

Once this has occurred, you or the attorney will sign the completion paper, called a "final deed".

In France it is called an "acte authentique", in Spain and Portugal an "escritura" and in Italy a "rogito".

After completion, the notary pays the taxes and registration fees. Any unpaid taxes or debts payable by the vendor are paid off by the notary

Before he hands the net sale proceeds to the seller, a few months may go by, and retention is always made by the notary, especially if the vendor is a foreigner.

Note that, unlike in England, where once you have registered the property in your name you receive the title deeds back (unless there is a mortgage, in which case the deeds are stored with the lender),)in foreign countries the notary acts as the holder of the deeds and you will never get the original deed back. All you will receive is a "certified copy".

If you have taken out a mortgage, you will then pay your first repayment and any condominium or community charges, together with ongoing taxes and costs.

Chapter 5
Currency Conversion and Buying at the Best Rates

So you've chosen the property and your pounds are sitting in your bank account waiting to be exchanged in Euros.

Banks vs FX Traders

Who do you use...? A high street bank or an FX broker? What is a currency broker?

A currency broker is a person who buys large quantities of currency, thereby being able to sell at a better rate. The broker will buy big and sell for smaller profits than the banks.

Make sure the broker is licensed and regulated by the FCA, as each must be nowadays. Check that the team is trained in buying at good rates and not just a telephone salesperson. Ask about sales personnel turnover.

Always compare currency brokers before signing up. Always ask questions.

Never use high street banks to exchange your monies. It's a well-known fact that you will achieve higher and better rates of exchange with FX companies than the banks.

"No Commission" is a Lie!

Banks have to make commission to survive. All they do is give you a lower exchange rate which takes into consideration the commission you would otherwise have to pay.

Using a currency broker could save you up to £5k on a £500k purchase.

Most brokers can save you between 1 and 3% on bank rates.

Currency exchange fluctuations mean that unless you are an expert and you watch the markets continuously, you will miss out on positive fluctuations, which would result in you getting better value.

Forward Buying & Spot Rates

The solution is to use a currency broker. Currency brokers can fix rates for you up to 24 months ahead, which means you will buy at that fixed rate and so make the most of your pound.

They can "forward buy" and "spot rate".

Fixing the currency rate for up to 24 months is great if the exchange rate falls, but not so advantageous if the pound strengthens.

If you want to plan ahead, it's a way of knowing that your currency mortgage will be a fixed amount of sterling each month.

Using a currency broker allows you to protect yourself from adverse market volatility. So if you think the market will worsen, you can forward buy. This means you usually pay 10% of the amount you buy on signing the forward purchase contract and then pay the rest on completion.

Avoid dynamic currency conversions. That means never pay in US dollars if you have the choice; always use the local currency.

Check the online comparison websites. Some general tips on money:

When transferring money, do it through the correct channels.

We use and recommend <u>TorFX</u>, based in Cornwall, with whom we have had a long and wonderful relationship.

Notes of Caution

Avoid Western Union and other such like companies, which are prone to being used by fraudsters.

Don't pay money into an escrow account suggested by the other party, unless the escrow holder is a lawyer!

Don't give out your personal account information.

Always trust your instincts and your gut!

Chapter 6
Taxes on your Overseas Property

Here is a list of the taxes you may have to consider as a UK tax payer when buying property abroad:

Stamp Duty/Land Tax

This is payable on the purchase of second hand properties.

Local VAT

On new builds only.
On professional services rendered to you during the purchase or build.
On supplies and products bought.

Community or Condominium Tax

Local versions of our "council tax".

Wealth Tax

Wealth tax may be payable. This occurs if you become resident in that country. (Some countries levy this on worldwide assets, others only on the assets held in that country.)

Income Tax

Income tax on rental income varies from one country to another. (Check double taxation treaties between the UK and the country you earn rental income in.)

Capital Gains Tax

Capital gains tax on the sale of your property. (It's usually the case that if you own your property for more than 4 years and 364 days you will avoid capital gains tax abroad. It gets less for every year of ownership. (Check as each country varies. In Morocco and Egypt no CGT is payable after 10 years.)

Remember..... that to be able to claim any capital gains tax reductions, you need to keep receipts and proof of purchases. If you attempt to claim a reduction in capital gains tax without one, because you have lost the receipt or proof of payment, or because the supplier has been paid in cash with no receipt, you won't get it!

If you are UK resident and you sell your home abroad, you may not be liable to CGT abroad, but you will, more than likely, have to pay CGT in the UK.

Again, double taxation treaties may exist, between the UK and the country in which you sell your home, which may reduce your UK CGT liability.

Inheritance Tax

In foreign countries it is usually the beneficiary who is liable for IHT, not the estate as in the UK. IHT is payable on your worldwide assets. (If you are tax resident in Italy, no IHT applies.)

If you are tax resident in the UK and derive rental income from your overseas property, you will pay income tax in the UK and in the country where the property is situated (subject to double taxation treaties, which are in place so you don't pay the full tax twice).

Late Payment "Penalty" Charges

These apply if you don't file accounts or pay taxes on time.

Foreign Country Taxation

Remember the following:

The purchase of a new build gives rise to VAT and not stamp duty

The purchase of a second hand property gives rise to stamp duty and land tax.

During ownership, you will pay local property taxes similar to our council taxes.

These local taxes go to maintaining highways, refuse collection and other local amenities such as police, fire, ambulance, hospitals and schools.

In most foreign countries, as a non-resident owner, you must have an accountant or fiscal adviser. This person will assist you to understand what tax you must pay and will liaise with your English tax adviser.

Once you retire abroad, you will be subject to the taxation of that country and no longer the UK, unless you continue to hold one or more assets, such as a rental property or bank account in the UK.

Tax Reliefs

Just like in the UK, every country will have a threshold before you start paying tax.

There will also be other exemptions and reliefs, which can be used to reduce annual taxation or capital gains tax on the sale of a business.

Do I Still Pay Tax in the United Kingdom, When I Move Abroad?

If you retire abroad and leave nothing in the UK, you will no longer pay tax in the UK; your new country of residence will ask you to pay tax.

Chapter 7
Estate Planning and
How to Structure your Purchase

Initial Considerations

Consider how you will buy before you do so. We all have different family situations, ranging from no parents, to a second wife and children from a previous marriage, or maybe you are part of a same sex marriage or relationship, known as a civil partnership.

Each one requires forethought as to how to buy and whether a company is required (such as in France where you can use a vehicle called an "SCI" to buy), thus paying no inheritance tax on death as the company owns the property and the deceased's shares are transferred, so as to avoid or at least minimise inheritance tax.

Some of the Choices Available to You:

Buying in the name of one person only.

Buying in joint names "in community of assets" (similar but not the same as joint tenancy or tenancy in common).

Buying as a joint venture partnership.

Civil partnership.

Off shore company incorporated in: Malta, Gibraltar, BVI, Hong Kong, USA, Cyprus and many more!).

Whether you use a company or other such vehicle will depend on the value of the property.

The higher the value the more you should consider using such a structure.

Assess your personal circumstances; current and future tax residency, lifestyle vs investment, purchase and duration of property ownership.

Co-ownership

You need to consider how you and your partner will hold the asset you are about to buy.

So is it to be joint tenancy or tenancy in common?........

These are English phrases, which must not be confused with the ways of owning what in England we call "estates in land". To use the English guidelines as anything more than that would be foolish!

Exercise caution when deciding to own property in "co-ownership", as described above.

In Italy, France, Spain and Portugal, for example, you have this concept of ownership which translated roughly says "in community", and it means you own the property with another or more persons. In Italy this is called "in comunione".

If you are married and you are buying with your spouse the notaio will enquire as to how you will hold the asset you are about to buy.

The choice is between "in regime di comunione dei beni" (jointly with the other spouse), or separately, which is termed "in regime di separazione dei beni".

We don't have the same distinction under English common law, per se.

For example, Italian law assumes you are in "comunione dei beni" unless you stipulate otherwise.

In England and Wales, you could only achieve this separation of assets by entering into a "pre-nuptial" agreement.

If you are in a partnership or a joint venture and are buying property, whether in England or abroad, always have a written agreement, which covers what will happen on sale, expulsion, and retirement or death. It should always cover who pays for what, as well as profit sharing and how this is to be calculated.

Be careful of second marriages and previous spouses, as well as children of the first marriage, who, in certain countries such as France, may still have rights on your property after your death.

Making a UK Will & a Foreign Will

However you buy, you must make an English will for all your UK assets and a foreign will, for your foreign assets.

Take care, because, in European countries, you can have "public wills", "private wills" and self-written "holograph wills".

A "holograph" will is one that is written in the handwriting of the testator. It cannot be written on a PC and then just executed and witnessed by two witnesses. Doing so automatically invalidates the will.

A public will is a will that a notary prepares for you; you execute it with witnesses and he then keeps it. And after death he publishes the will.

The private will is written by a person as before, but he then hands the notary the written will and he keeps it until the testator's death. On death he publishes the will.

Evaluate succession planning, inheritance planning and required flexibility.

CHANGES IN EU SUCCESSION LAW: EFFECTIVE AS OF 17TH AUGUST 2015

On 17th August 2015, new rules, known as the "BRUSSELS IV" Regulation, number 650/2012, came into force.

The effect of these new rules, which bind 25 of the 28 EU members, is that citizens in those 25 countries can choose the law, which will apply to the distribution of the estate or assets they leave behind, upon death.

These new rules, embodied in the new Regulation 650/2012, have been debated since 2012 and are meant to simplify the procedures for dealing with the distribution of property, where the deceased dies in one country, with assets in another EU country.
The aim of the "Brussels IV" Regulation is to allow a "European Certificate of Succession, [ECS] to be issued by the country of the person's habitual residence, which must be accepted and

recognised in all other EU states.

It aims to unify European succession rules, so that, as international lawyers, we no longer have to obtain a Grant of Probate here in the UK, then have it translated, legalised and notarised with the Hague Convention Apostille, by the Foreign and Commonwealth Office, which will then allows the English probate to be recognised abroad and in so recognising the document [in this case the English will] recognising the wishes of the deceased person, although strictly speaking in the past, up to the 17th August 2015, if you were English and had a property abroad, the law of the foreign country, in which the property was situated, should have been applied.

I say 25 countries, because the UK, Ireland and Holland have "opted out" from the rules having to be applied to property in those three countries. This means, that if you are English or from the UK, then you cannot choose, say French Law, to govern the administration of your house in London. The Courts here in England will only distribute assets in England and Wales, according to English Law.

The new rules can, however, be used by a citizen of one of the three "opt out" countries, when dealing with their foreign assets, such as a property in France.

So, this means that if you are English," domiciled" in England and you have a property in France, you can either choose your country of "habitual residence", let's call it, the one you usually live in, or your nationality, to govern the administration of your estate upon death.

The problem is that, for English citizens, the Law of England and Wales does not recognise the concept of "habitual residence". Our laws only recognise the concept of "domicile", which is divided into three types. **Beware: the two concepts are very different.**

The English person making an English will, which covers foreign property **must expressly declare in the will,** the country of "habitual residence" or "nationality", that he wishes to apply, in the distribution of the FOREIGN [NOT UK] property.

By expressly stating in the will, that the laws applicable to the deceased's "nationality" apply on his death, this avoids any doubt or discussion on what is meant by "habitual residence" and the concept of "Renvoi" [or where one national court sends a matter to another country's national court, to decide upon a point of law].

Chapter 8
Becoming a Professional
Foreign Property Investor

So you've bought your first property, and after 6 months you have the burning desire to do it all over again, as your first experience went really well with Kobalt Law LLP's expert help!

I'm not going to repeat all the "legals", as well as taxation aspects and which structures might be best for you. Imagine I had just repeated them all.

Investing as a professional foreign property investor is no less difficult than doing it in the UK.

Remember, there are very few "safe" investments, only "opportunities"!

Why Do It?

People become professional investors to gain "financial freedom", to work when they like, as they like and from where they like. They have decided to go from a "job" mentality to a "business ownership" mentality.

It's a fact of life that we work longer and longer, for a lesser reward, and in the process become totally stressed...a great recipe for a long and healthy life.

The ingredients and strategies required to become a successful investor abroad are the same, believe or not!
The only five real changes are:

1. The property or land is in a foreign country.
2. The language is different.
3. The law is different.
4. The market economics are particular to that country.
5. Exchange rate fluctuations.

As with all such matters, you need to sit down, with a blank piece of paper and set out the reasons why you want to invest, ultimate goals for the investments and how much you have at your disposal.

Choice of Country

In the early 2000's, the pioneers of professional international property investment chose the former communist countries like Poland, Romania, the Czech Republic, Hungary and Bulgaria.

I think it's fair to say that the only ones I would still go for from that list are Poland, Hungary and Bulgaria. All still have advantages to investing in them.

For example, Poland is full of castles, which can be bought for next to nothing and which are then eligible for substantial EU grants to modernise them as hotels with golf courses, offering good rates of return of 7% upwards.

Hungary is currently attracting foreign investors, as it has a fixed rate of income tax (16% at the time of going to print, whether you trade as a sole trader or a company). The returns on investment are currently 6 to 8 % and there are less ante money laundering requirements, making the opening of bank accounts and the ability to trade easier.

Bargains are still to be had in Sofia, the capital of Bulgaria, with similar rates of return.

Considerations Which will Apply

However, these examples aside, the usual practice of"first in... first out" with good returns still applies.

The usual suspects, closer to home, such as France, Spain, Italy and Portugal are still the best and simplest to deal with.

Whatever the reason for choosing a country, ensure you always do the required amount of pre-purchase "due diligence".

Check past fluctuations in property prices and changes in trends.

Such trends are very often dictated by supply and demand and other economic factors, such as rates of tax applicable, interest rates, stability of the market generally, unemployment, emigration and immigration.

Other factors are those surrounding international sports events, such as the world cup, world athletics and the Olympics.

We all saw this in Beijing, where western based investors bought in the areas surrounding Beijing. These apartments were used by the athletes and then they were bought by investors and rented out to the open market.

A similar phenomenon has occurred in our London Olympic Village in Stratford, in the east end of London.

Here, the Olympic park, now known as "the Queen Elizabeth Park", has been sold, partly to private investors and partly used as social housing. The first investors in made good returns.

Check if the country you want to invest in has adequate land areas, ripe for development, or whether developable land is limited. The latter will have the desired effect of "sky rocketing" prices.

Other important considerations are; a government's view on planning and development and what transport links it will build to a newly developed area. Trends such as taste and fashion, the advent of budget airlines and the "el Niño" effect may also play a role in choice of investment.

Category of Investment

As I have said previously, consider your exit strategy before you buy. Consider whether it will it be easy to offload the investment at the right price.

Next consider the type of investment you want to go for. Long term or short term?

Will you invest in a second hand property, a new development, timeshare, fractional ownership or maybe an aparthotel?

Whatever you invest in, you should always try to buy at "below market value" (known as "BMV").

Be careful that the BMV is correctly calculated, not artificial, and that it's not just a marketing technique used by a developer or agent to draw you into a bad deal!

How will you Finance the Investment?

Will you use your own money or a lender's? Will you leverage using a mortgage?

The answer is clearly that if you can get a mortgage, use the bank's money and not your own!.

Will you put a small sum down or a large sum?

Will you actually put any money down at all?

Serious investors don't use their own money… in fact, where possible, they don't use any money at all!!

How do they do that, you ask?

Deals are all around you and it's just a case of being able to spot them. This is how serious investors, in the UK property market, make millions.

I'm not going to go through all the various options, over and above the obvious investment strategies we all know, and some of which I have touched on in this book, but I will describe some interesting investment strategies below.

The usual way to build an investment portfolio is to use your own money or raise finance to buy and then let the investment produce an income yield.

"Control" vs "Ownership"

Many serious investors don't do this. Smart thinking coupled with lenders now being very risk averse and not lending in the wild way they used to, pre 2008, lead such investors to choose to "control" an asset, rather than to "own" it.

I use the words "control" and "ownership" very carefully.

Once you have "control" or maybe "ownership" of your investment (dependent on whether you have actually bought the house, villa or apartment, or whether you are still on "contract", yet to complete), you need to decide whether you will "long term" or "short term" let or whether you will sell your contract on ("assign") to a third party, so they can complete the purchase, sometime in the future and you just make a quick, but smaller profit, usually.

This lets you exit quickly into the next deal.

How do they "control" rather than "own" an asset, as an investment strategy?

The "Motivated Seller"

Well, what they do is they find what's known in the profession as "a motivated seller".

What is "a motivated seller"? This is a person who, for whatever reason, needs to offload a property or a development or a piece of land, quickly.

This may be as a result of impending bankruptcy, divorce, change in market economics, a bank foreclosure, emigration and a number of other reasons.

As you can see, a" motivated seller" is very rarely in a "good place".
You might say that's taking advantage of such a person.

Well, I suppose you could say what's good for one person isn't good for another. You are resolving a huge problem for the seller

You need to be awake to these "deals".

Having found your "motivated seller" you can proceed in one of a few different ways.

You could use a "lease option" agreement or a "rent to buy" agreement.

Each one works in a different way.

Although both could end up in you owning the property, you may decide, whichever you use, that when you have to make a decision as to whether you complete the transaction, you might not, based on the then current market value of the property.

Using "Lease Options" & "Rent to Buy Options"

A "lease option" works on the basis that the owner, who wants to sell, is cash strapped. He cannot afford the monthly mortgage repayments. So, to assist him you enter into a lease option. You agree to take over his monthly mortgage repayments. An option fee is payable. It can range from £1 to £10,000 or any other sum agreed by the parties.

Ideally you want the owner to leave the premises. This is called a "sandwich option". You then install your own tenant, who pays more than the mortgage repayment. The result is, you pay the mortgage and are left with a surplus to cover any expenditure.

The tenant will then purchase the property from you, in say, 10 years' time, at the end of the option agreement. He will pay you a higher purchase price than the price you have agreed to pay the current owner. You enter into a future sale agreement with the tenant and manage the property under a management agreement. The outgoing owner grants you a power of attorney to deal with the property on his behalf.

This leaves you with a capital gain and having received an income throughout the term of the agreement.

The price you pay the departing owner is one agreed at today's rates and values, so that any increase in the market value belongs to you and not the departing owner.

Another way is to use the "rent to buy" agreement. This is usually used where a vendor wants to sell, but can't find a willing or "motivated buyer", who has the full purchase price in one lump sum. This is due nowadays to banks not wanting to lend. It's also called "vendor finance".

This kind of agreement has now been legislated for, in most European countries, so as to energise the stagnant property markets.

The agreement lasts up to 10 years, and in essence the purchaser becomes the tenant and pays an initial premium plus a monthly sum (usually the total agreed price divided by the number of months of the agreement).

The last payment acts as an "option fee". The parties then attend the notary and complete the transfer from the vendor to the purchaser and pay the transfer taxes and registration fees.

The purchaser can sublease it out to another, as long as the monthly amounts are paid. Again, he can rent it out for a higher amount than that which he is paying the vendor.

At the end of the option period, if he doesn't want to complete, he could sell to a third party at a higher price, and make a capital gain.

The "Leaseback" Strategy

The last example of a more straightforward investment concerns France.

As I mentioned earlier in this chapter, France has always had a strong investment sector for the foreign property investor, who wants no or very little occupation time in the unit he buys.

This involves a concept called "leaseback".

This is achieved by buying from a developer, who has registered with the government, to develop and build in a designated "holiday & tourism area".

The units are then sold to foreign investors on what is called a "leaseback" scheme".

The French have been very good at developing this scheme for many years.

The advantages to the foreign investor are that, as soon as he completes the purchase, his unit is then rented to a tour operator for a recurring lease of 9 or 11 years (unless the owner breaks the lease and does not renew it).

The tour operator takes full "control" of the unit and rents it out to you and me, when we buy a package holiday through "Thomsons" or "First Choice".

This guarantees you a true return.

It is not a "guaranteed return" that some developers offer you, where you actually pay a higher purchase price, part of which is your own "guaranteed return". So, in effect, in such a case, you get back what you've just paid in!

There are substantial tax advantages with the leaseback scheme, as you recover all the VAT back (on a proportionate basis), from the French government, as long as if you leave it in the scheme for 20 years of more.

If you exit before, then you must repay some VAT. The capital gains, on exiting this scheme, have also been proved to be higher than other investments in France.

Whichever scheme or strategy you use, it has to fit your way of life and your expectations.

My simple advice is to research the topic well and then go for it (subject to all my tips!).

Chapter 9
Retiring Abroad

The word "retirement" conjures up different thoughts in different people's minds, ranging from total lethargy, to jumping out of a plane at 20,000 feet!

Today's "retiree" is much younger, fitter, healthier, and active, gets bored more quickly and doesn't want to let go of their youth quite so easily, as in generations past.

With the stresses and strains of city life, travel to and from work getting worse, the daily grind at work and the thought of that holiday in 9 months' time, many are resorting to selling up and moving abroad permanently for a total lifestyle change.

The ability to carry on most jobs and professions abroad, with the recognition of qualifications and the advent of fantastic technology, such as the world wide net, the mobile, the ipad, the PC, email and the ease with which a person can now work from home, drives many forward thinking people to swap the daily routine for a better life abroad.

What advantages are there to moving abroad?......Not only a life of sunshine and better weather, but also a life where, as a "retiree" you can work in a different way, have fun, meet many different people, from all over the world, opening your horizons, but also work in a smarter way, which drives a greater profit into your pocket.

It is now the case that the government pushes the age at which it will pay you your accrued state pension ever higher, always placing it just out of reach and always leaving less in the pot, making it impossible to live on that alone.

Some have sold up and have substantial funds to live on, which, given time, will dwindle, if not topped up. Others are young enough to start a new life, either as an entrepreneur, or in paid employment.

People now see "retirement" in a different way; no longer the end of life, but the dawn of a new era.

The country you choose to retire to will dictate how well or otherwise you will integrate into local society. I am happy to say that statistics show integration of foreigners is best in Italy!

Remember that when you move abroad, whether to retire or just as a holiday home, you will benefit from making friends with the neighbours and the local community. Get involved and show you care.
You will soon see how many friends and acquaintances you make.

Remember......... what you sow, you reap!

Retiring abroad, even to places like Bulgaria, is no longer a question of moving to the third world. Such countries are much more developed than 20 years ago, having received EU regional and national funding. This ensures stronger infrastructure and all-round better transportation.

Telephone and postal systems have been upgraded and I was amazed to see that, in some rural areas of Italy, they seem to have stronger internet capacity than we do in London!

Choose a country that has cheap flights from regional and national airports and cities that are well-connected by rail.

Land and property is cheaper abroad compared to the UK, despite increases in values over the last decade. You can get much more for your money abroad, and much more interesting structures you can shape and work with, especially if you're setting up a business.

Fresh produce is of a higher quality and nutritional content.

Like anything, as I said earlier, you have to work at relationships with new people.

You have to be prepared to learn the language and to make mistakes. You will be more easily accepted if you try to learn the language, rather than to persist in English.

There is a change in culture to take in. This ranges from the daily newscasts, to the restaurants, to the way people treat you in banks and shops, and the way the police look at you and how you must talk to them.

Claiming your UK Pension Abroad

Retiring abroad means you will have to register with the local authorities and the doctor, and you need to open a bank account to receive and pay money from, such as your income and your pension.

UK pensions (including war pensions) can be paid to you within the European Economic Area (greater than the EU); however, pension credits cannot be paid outside the UK. You can also obtain a pension forecast from the UK government. You cannot usually be paid the majority of UK benefits if you are permanently resident abroad; however, you should be able to claim the equivalent benefit abroad.

If your pension is a UK armed forces' pension, you will be taxed in the UK, not in Italy. All other kinds of pensions are taxed in Italy and not in the UK. If you receive any pension lump sum whilst abroad, it will be taxed according to the tax laws of the country you now reside in. If you receive this before you leave the UK, then you will pay UK tax on it.

Emigrating or retiring to Europe no longer means you can avoid or evade taxation! The tax authorities are now very much experts in locating people who decide to avoid tax.

The weather and climatic conditions will play a significant role in the location you choose, both from retirement and /or a business. This may range from high altitude mountainous regions for walking and snow related activities, to sea level resorts, such as in southern Italy, where the temperature in July and August hits above 40 degrees.

When you decide to retire abroad, you need to prepare a check list, well in advance of all the considerations to take stock of, before, during and after the move. Although many of the matters you will write down on the list will be the same for everyone, such as removals, doctors, hospitals and schools, some may be particular to the region or the type of business you may be setting up.

The first thing I would urge you to do… don't buy straightaway!

Organise a trial period in a property, as a 6 -12 months rental. You will get a better feeling as to whether you like and whether the whole "retiring abroad" thing is for you or not.

This is because 70% of the people who move abroad and buy straightaway end up either returning to the UK or moving to another region. This only means more legal and other associated fees, flowing out of your pocket into others'!

Agree on a short term rental and if you like the place you try, ask the owner whether he will knock the rent you pay off the purchase price, if you exercise an "option to buy".

Rent to Buy

I mentioned, in the last chapter, this new European phenomenon," rent to buy"; developed to stimulate many countries' stagnant property markets, as well as allowing purchasers to avoid the problem of banks not lending, as they once used to.

Here follows a more detailed overview of this strategy:

So, if I have a house and I can't find a buyer with the money to purchase the property, I can find a willing, motivated buyer, who does not have enough to pay for an outright purchase, but who has enough for a deposit and to pay me a monthly rent, which will be deducted from the eventual purchase price at the end of the term. This is, in effect, a "lease option" scheme, as is becoming more prevalent in the UK, for the same reasons.

The parties enter into a rental purchase agreement, which is usually no longer than 10 years.

The owner moves out and the purchaser becomes a long-term tenant, paying the monthly rent, which reduces the purchase price, with each monthly payment. At the end of the term, come the agreed time to exercise the option to buy, the tenant can do so in writing and the last calendar payment is used as the option fee.

The parties then attend the "notaio", for example, in Italy and sign the rogito, or final sale deed, which transfers ownership to the buyer.

During the rental period, the tenant will be responsible for the upkeep of the property, but substantial repairs are down to the owner, who can then charge interest on the monies he has had to pay out, in respect of the repairs or renovations.

If the tenant breaches the rental agreement, the worst case scenario is that he loses all the monies he has paid and has to leave the property.

The owner gets the property back, without having to recompense the tenant.

This type of "lease purchase" scheme is prevalent in many European countries, where governments have made the required legislative rule changes to accommodate such schemes.

Short term and long term rentals, in most countries, are governed by different rules and regulations. Take care that you don't create a long term tenancy by renewing a short term tenancy over and over again, thus granting the tenant rights you would not otherwise want him to acquire.

There are other ways of "owning" or "occupying" property, such as time sharing or home exchanges. I don't recommend either.

You should also have a good command of how to use a PC and the internet; before you leave and when you arrive in your new country, you must acquire a local email address.

Before leaving the UK permanently, you must advise the pensions department in Newcastle and give them your new bank account details.

Applying for Residence in your New Country

Remember that, if you move within the European Union, from another EU state, you have the automatic right of freedom, movement of goods and services, and right to reside.

This does not, however, mean you can move without completing the particular country's requirements for obtaining residence there. This is usually done by visiting the local police station or online in more developed countries.

"Residence" is applied for by filling the forms, proving ID, together with photos and usually proof of funds, that you have a job or are self-employed and that you have registered with the local chamber of commerce.

You must prove that you will not be a burden on the state.

In most countries you must register for a tax or fiscal code number, very similar to our tax number or social security number. This puts you on the taxman's and government's radar.

You cannot buy land or property without this number. The number, once obtained, lasts forever.

You can then apply for an identity card at some point as a permanent resident.

Remember to register with the consulate or the embassy.

Persons from outside the EU do not have the same entrenched rights as those from within the EU. They must apply for a long stay visa, which may then lead to an equivalent of the UK system of "indefinite leave to remain".

If you have animals, which you wish to take, these must have a passport, be vaccinated and be electronically chipped.

Have a Clear Out & Create a List

Come the day when you want to move, don't take all your unused "stuff" with you! Sell it beforehand, online, using eBay or Gumtree, or have a house sale or table top sale.

Your list of matters to consider must start with how affordable is it to live there.

Compare costs of luxury foods, drink, staple foods, clothes, repairs, furniture, reading materials and car costs.

Moving to Europe is not the same as moving round the world to Australia and New Zealand. You can't jump on a plane or train and be there in 2 hours! You will leave family and friends behind and may not be able to see them for long periods, due to work or cost of travel.

If you can, leave a "pied a terre" in the UK, even if you leave permanently, just in case you have to come back quickly, for unforeseen circumstances.

Do you Take the Right Hand Drive Car?

Consider whether you will take your right hand drive car with you or sell it and buy one in the country of destination. Buying cars abroad is much more difficult and convoluted than buying one in the UK. It usually means the attendance at a notary's office to seal the deal, especially if buying a second hand car. Remember overtaking in a right hand drive car is more dangerous in left hand drive countries.

You cannot keep the car for more than 12 months in a foreign country without changing the number plate over to a local registration, which might mean you also having to pay VAT on the value of the car.

This also goes for your UK driving licence. If you stay in a European country for more than 12 months, you must exchange your UK driving licence for a licence of the new country.

New insurance is also required, unless you extend coverage to foreign countries.

Don't forget to apply your international driving licence, well before you drive, to cover you in the interim.

Remember also that foreign countries require you to carry anti-glare headlight lenses (for right hand drive cars) spare bulbs, sometimes a breathalyser kit (France), high visibility jacket, blanket, triangle first aid kit and spare driving glasses (Spain).

If you leave permanently, after 183 nights out of the UK you will automatically become a tax resident in your new country.

Avoid two tax demands by telling the UK tax authority that you have left permanently.

Learning the Language

Learn the language by attending a local class or by having one to one private tuition, well before you emigrate, and continue this once you arrive... Pick up a CD or "Rosetta" course to keep it up.

Watch the TV in the new country's language and listen to the radio, as you have to strain to understand what's being said since you can't see the person's lips moving.

If you are single, find a partner and maybe marry them!.

What to Do before you Leave the UK

Start by cancelling all direct debits and standing orders. Notify your bank of the departure.

Close the account if necessary, although I would just keep it open.

Arrange for your UK pension to be paid abroad.

Medical & Health Issues

If you are in the EU and are from the EU, take your European health insurance card with you. This covers you for the first three months.

This covers 90% of treatment costs, and these should be free.

If they aren't, you first have to pay for the treatment and the visit and then recover those costs when you return to the UK.

For the first three months of your stay abroad you can continue to travel back and use the UK system for free.

The majority of doctors and dentists within the EU are private paid professionals and you usually have to pay them there and then!

Medical records cannot be physically taken, but your new doctor can get access to them from abroad.

I would advise to take out international medical insurance such as BUPA international.

After the first three months, you will have to register with a local GP.

If you are entitled to state benefits, you need to fill in the appropriate forms, so the UK can tell the other EU country that you are entitled to free assistance and drugs; you are then entitled to the same assistance as a local person.

If you retire and you have paid your national insurance contributions in the UK, you will also be entitled to the same level of cover as locals.

Don't forget to take advantage of pensioner discounts and benefits, and to claim them.

Crime & Other Issues

Crime, such as petty theft, burglary, muggings and such also vary from one country to the other. Crime rates in mainland Europe are higher than in the UK, because of the ability of gangs to get in quick and then retreat to another country overnight. Take care when walking in unlit places or at night, through parks. Always take a friend and don't attract unwanted attention.

Lock your home as you would in the UK and be aware that in certain countries, like Spain, foreign gangs, usually from Bulgaria and Romania, prey on foreign owners, sometimes gassing them as they sleep, only for them to wake up and find that they have been completely stripped of all their belongings. This happened in August 2015 to Jenson Button and his wife on the French Riviera! I suggest you fit bars and security screens, cameras, sensors and other detection equipment.

Other types of crime occur online, just as they do in the UK. Be careful of this online fraud.

If you have to go into a care home, you have a choice of a fully private home or one which is a mixture of part private and part state aided.

Most EU countries have the concepts of, home carers, meals on wheels, companion services and centres for the elderly.

On the more practical level, beware of biting insects and reptiles, which will vary from country to country, region to region and city to city.

As regards mental illness, the quality of care and assistance varies substantially from one country to another. If you have a pre-existing medical or psychological condition, it pays to see what help exists in that country before you move there. Don't forget to get your mail forwarded on to yourself, for at least 12 months.

Obtain various quotes for removals and make sure they quote "like for like". Some cover packing for you, others not.
Some include one type of insurance, but not another. Choose one, which is known for international removals; such as "Bishop's Move", "Pickfords", "Britannia" and many more. Choose one that has an office in the country you are moving to, if possible.

Make a list of what to take and what you won't take, and remember that the electricity supply is different abroad. You will have to take electric adaptors until you get the UK plugs changed over.

Each country has different voltages. Take care because most European countries don't have an earth, in the socket, like we do on the plug; just neutral and live.

Finally, cancel the milk, the newspapers and other monthly subscriptions, such as the gym, and return library books.

Take meter readings for final readings or if you are renting out.

If you have an alarm contract, notify them that a new person is moving into the property and authorise the alarm company personnel, in writing, to talk to them.

Pay up all outstanding bills and utilities.

Remember, that for up to 15 years from the year you leave the UK, you can continue to vote in parliamentary and EU elections, if you are registered correctly.

You are then ready to retire abroad!
Check that your passport is valid!

Sometimes it Doesn't Work Out .... Returning Home... What to Do

Although it is true to say that many people stay and enjoy life in their new home, for many, it turns out not to be what they were looking for.

The reasons are many. I'm hoping that by following my tips and putting my advice into practice, you will be one of the lucky ones.

Remember....... "Proper planning prevents poor performance"... (usually!)!

Some of the many reasons why people might have to return home may be:

One of the two partners is less enthusiastic about the move.

One partner may die or become ill unexpectedly.

The money may run out

The business may become insolvent.

Unreal expectations

When this happens, you have to work backwards to unravel all the preparation you made in the first place.

You may need to sell, or at least in the "short term" rent the home out.

You will have to notify the tax and pension authorities of the country you are leaving that this is the case.

You will have to make contact with an estate agent to sell or rent your property out and thereafter manage it, in your absence.

Obtain a couple of valuations, if you have to sell.

Check the market.

Perhaps you have made so many acquaintances in your time there that you can sell it without an agent and without having to pay him commission.

Remember, you may have to pay capital gains and other taxes on the sale.

You will certainly have to pay notary fees and VAT.

Create a list of matters to attend to upon return to the UK.

Do you still have a UK bank account?

Contact the tax authorities. Contact the pensions' department.

Re-register with your GP.

Check that your passport is still valid.

Do you need to buy an exit visa?

Give a forwarding address.

Ensure pets can still travel to avoid quarantine.

Chapter 10
Starting your Own Business Abroad

Let's start from the point in time that you are correctly registered in your new country and are able either to be employed or become self-employed.

You've decided to risk self-employment.

In any country, there are certain basic requirements, over and above those we have mentioned, before you can start your new venture.

You will usually have to do the following, although this is a non-exhaustive list:

Set up a local company to trade through
Register with the local tax authority
Open a bank account
Join a trade association for particular professions
Have your qualifications recognised (lawyer, doctor, architect, dentist etc.)
Find premises unless you start from home
Have tenancy agreement looked at by a local lawyer
Have employment contract templates prepared
Find an accountant
Find a local tax representative ("commercialista" in Italy, "gestoria" in Spain)
Obtain public liability insurance

A New Business vs an Existing Business?

If you're buying an existing business, you must carry out all the required due diligence that you would in the UK. Use local professionals, to help.

It's far easier to buy one that's already trading. You can buy it and keep the old owner on for a while to teach you the trade and show you the ropes. Insert such a clause into the contract so you can keep him on.

Never buy a business without a thoroughly comprehensive legal contract, in writing.

Never do anything on the shake of a hand or with the contract drafted "on the back of a fag packet!"

Check three years' accounts, if the business is that old.

Ask questions.

Don't be afraid; it's your money and your life.

Starting a New Venture

Prepare a proper realistic business plan.

Choose one of the many trading structures that may exist (ranging from sole trader, different types of limited company, partnerships, and finally the equivalent of a joint stock company or a plc).

Don't forget the legal and accountancy assistance.

I would also talk to local banks, if you need local finance.

Choose the correct location for the business.

Does it need passing trade, such as a bar or restaurant, or will a first floor office suffice?

How do you hire local staff and check them out?

Will your business be governed by specific rules and regulations?

You cannot, in many countries, just go online and buy an "off the shelf company" as we can in the UK.

You will have to go to a local notary, who will create and write the memorandum and articles of the company. Factor in the time that this will take; possibly a month.

Just as in the UK, there are many different types of companies and other kinds of trading vehicles, some similar to our "partnerships" and "LLPs"

Beware of illegal opening hours and overworking staff, more than the permitted number of hours per week.

Always ensure that the employees sign a letter of offer and a contract of employment, which sets out all the salary and benefits. The following should be covered in it as a minimum:

(job title and specification, holidays, sick and other leave health insurance, union membership, probationary periods, confidentiality, medical examinations, travel expenses, relocation packages, flexi time and overtime, a restraint of trade clause and non-competition clause). Leave nothing to chance. Provide adequate training and refresher courses.

Check what licences and permits you may need for the importation of raw materials and other unfinished or finished products.

Check the local VAT rates.

Some countries class certain jobs as "regulated professions".

We do this here in the UK for Solicitors, barristers, doctors, dentists, architects and surveyors.

You will have to show you have a valid accreditation from your country of origin, to call yourself whatever it is you want to do, and that your professional qualifications are recognised by the country, in question.

The French are notorious for refusing to recognise foreign qualifications!

This is notwithstanding the fact that such rights are enshrined within the EU treaty.

You may have them recognised but you may have to perform a period of training, to upgrade your knowledge.

Beware that you use the correct business etiquette and correspondence.

Assume nothing!
Question everything.
Learn the proper skills and language.
Learn how to meet and greet.

Learn the correct forms of negotiations and avoid chauvinism. Always keep your accounts up to date and pay your taxes on time to avoid late filing or payment penalties.

Selling the Business On

When you have had enough or you just want to change direction you can sell your business.

You could sell just the goodwill, or the goodwill, fixtures and fittings, and the property itself

Take local accountancy advice first.

If you sell the building, use the services of an estate agent.

Ensure you have up to date accounts and that the previous years' accounts are all up to date, before you get the buyer looking and asking questions you cannot answer!

Have all your papers tidy and ready for inspection.

Instruct a notary to prepare the sale contract.

Have the business valued beforehand so you know how much to ask for!

Have the stock in trade valued.

Create a list of all tangible assets (plant and machinery) as well and intangible assets (intellectual property, consisting of patents and copyrights etc).

Don't forget to have these valued!

Ensure that your designs and other intellectual property have been protected to maintain the intrinsic value.

Once the sale has been completed, your accountant will tell you the taxation payable and what's left in the pot!

You may have contracted to stay on for a while. After that, you're free!!

Chapter 11
Brexit: The Future After the UK Leaves Europe

The Current Position

The UK has voted to leave the European Union. It is scheduled to depart at 11pm UK time on Friday 29 March, 2019. The UK and EU have provisionally agreed on the three "divorce" issues of how much the UK owes the EU, what happens to the Northern Ireland border and what happens to UK citizens living elsewhere in the EU and EU citizens living in the UK. Talks are now moving on to future relations - after agreement was reached on a 21-month "transition" period to smooth the way to post-Brexit relations.

The 'Transition' Period

It refers to a period of time after 29 March, 2019, to 31 December, 2020, to get everything in place and allow businesses and others to prepare for the moment when the new post-Brexit rules between the UK and the EU begin. It also allows more time for the details of the new relationship to be fully hammered out. Free movement will continue during the transition period, as the EU wanted. The UK will be able to strike its own trade deals - although they won't be able to come into force until 1 January 2021.

What will happen in the Future?

Negotiations about future relations between the UK and the EU are just beginning. Both sides hope they can agree within six months on the outline of future relations on things like trade, travel and security. If all goes to plan this deal could then be given the go ahead by both sides in time for 29 March 2019. Theresa May delivered a big speech setting out her thoughts on the UK and EU's future relations on 2 March, 2018.
So will Brexit definitely happen?
The UK government and the main UK opposition party both say Brexit will happen.

Why is Britain leaving the European Union?

A referendum - a vote in which everyone (or nearly everyone) of voting age can take part - was held on Thursday 23 June, 2016, to decide whether the UK should leave or remain in the European Union. Leave won by 51.9% to 48.1%. The referendum turnout was 71.8%, with more than 30 million people voting.

What was the breakdown across the UK?

England voted for Brexit, by 53.4% to 46.6%. Wales also voted for Brexit, with Leave getting 52.5% of the vote and Remain 47.5%. Scotland and Northern Ireland both backed staying in the EU. Scotland backed Remain by 62% to 38%, while 55.8% in Northern Ireland voted Remain and 44.2% Leave.

What changed in government after the referendum?

Theresa May the new Prime Minister and the former home secretary took over from David Cameron, who announced he was resigning on the day he lost the referendum. She became

PM without facing a full Conservative leadership contest after her key rivals from what had been the Leave side pulled out.

Where does Theresa May stand on Brexit?

Theresa May was against Brexit during the referendum campaign but is now in favour of it because she says it is what the British people want. Her key message has been that "Brexit means Brexit" and she triggered the two year process of leaving the EU on 29 March, 2017. She set out her negotiating goals in a letter to the EU council president Donald Tusk. She outlined her plans for a transition period after Brexit in a big speech in Florence, Italy. She then set out her thinking on the kind of trading relationship the UK wants with the EU, in a speech in March 2018.

Brexit Negotiations

They officially started a year after the referendum, on 19 June, 2017.

The UK and EU negotiating teams met face-to-face for one week each month, with a few extra sessions also thrown in ahead of EU summits. Their first tasks were trying to get an agreement on the rights of UK and EU expat citizens after Brexit, reaching a figure for the amount of money the UK will need to pay on leaving, the so-called "divorce bill", and what happens to the Northern Ireland border. A provisional deal on these issues was reached on 8 December: They then agreed terms for the "transition" phase and now have moved on to the permanent post-Brexit relationship.

What is the European Union?

The European Union - often known as the EU - is an economic and political partnership involving 28 European countries). It began after World War Two to foster economic co-operation, with the idea that countries which trade together are more likely to avoid going to war with each other.

It has since grown to become a "single market" allowing goods and people to move around, basically as if the member states were one country. It has its own currency, the euro, which is used by 19 of the member countries, its own parliament and it now sets rules in a wide range of areas - including on the environment, transport, consumer rights and even things such as mobile phone charges.

What is Article 50?

Article 50 is a plan for any country that wishes to exit the EU to do so. It was created as part of the Treaty of Lisbon - an agreement signed up to by all EU states which became law in 2009. Before that treaty, there was no formal mechanism for a country to leave the EU.

Any EU member state may decide to quit the EU, that it must notify the European Council and negotiate its withdrawal with the EU, that there are two years to reach an agreement - unless everyone agrees to extend it - and that the exiting state cannot take part in EU internal discussions about its departure.

When is the UK due to leave the EU?

For the UK to leave the EU it had to invoke Article 50 of the Lisbon Treaty which gives the two sides two years to agree the terms of the split. Theresa May triggered this process on 29 March, meaning the UK is scheduled to leave at 11pm UK time on Friday, 29 March 2019. It can be extended if all 28 EU members agree, but at the moment all sides are focusing on that date as being the key one, and Theresa May is seeking to put it into British law.

What's going to happen to all the EU laws in force in the UK?

The Conservative government has introduced the European Union (Withdrawal) Bill to Parliament. If passed, it will end the primacy of EU law in the UK. This "Great Repeal Bill", as it was originally called, is supposed to incorporate all EU legislation into UK law in one lump, after which the government will decide over a period of time which parts to keep, change or remove. The government is facing claims from Remain supporting MPs that it is giving itself sweeping powers to change legislation without proper Parliamentary scrutiny.

What do 'soft' and 'hard' Brexit mean?

These terms are used during debate on the terms of the UK's departure from the EU. There is no strict definition of either, but they are used to refer to the closeness of the UK's relationship with the EU post-Brexit.

So at one extreme, "hard" Brexit could involve the UK refusing to compromise on issues like the free movement of people even if it meant leaving the single market or having to give up hopes of aspects of free trade arrangements. At the other end of the scale, a "soft" Brexit might follow a similar path to Norway, which is a member of the single market and has to accept the free movement of people as a result of that.

What is the single market?

The single market is seen by its advocates as the EU's biggest achievement and one of the main reasons it was set up in the first place. Britain was a member of a free trade area in Europe before it joined what was then known as the common market. In a free trade area countries can trade with each other without paying tariffs - but it is not a single market because the member states do not have to merge their economies together.

The European Union single market, which was completed in 1992, allows the free movement of goods, services, money and people within the European Union, as if it was a single country. It is possible to set up a business or take a job anywhere within it. The idea was to boost trade, create jobs and lower prices. But it requires common law-making to ensure products are made to the same technical standards and imposes other rules to ensure a "level playing field".

What is the difference between the single market and the customs union?

The customs union ensures EU member states all charge the same import duties to countries outside the EU. It allows member states to trade freely with each other, without burdensome customs checks at borders, but it limits their freedom to strike their own trade deals.

It is different from a free trade area. In a free trade area no tariffs, taxes or quotas are charged on goods and services moving within the area but members are free to strike their own external trade deals.

The single market is a very different beast - it is not just about the trade in goods. It allows the free movement of people, money and services as if the EU was a single country.
Who is negotiating Britain's exit from the EU?

Theresa May set up a government department, headed by veteran Conservative MP and Leave campaigner David Davis, to take responsibility for Brexit talks. Former defence secretary, Liam Fox, who also campaigned to leave the EU, was given the new job of international trade secretary and Boris Johnson, who was a leader of the official Leave campaign, is foreign secretary. These three are each playing roles in negotiations with the EU and seek out new international agreements, although Mrs May, as prime minister will play the key role.

How long will it take for Britain to leave the EU?

The Article 50 process lasts two years so the intention is for the UK to leave the EU on 29 March 2019. EU law still stands in the UK until it ceases being a member. As things stand there will not be a final break on that day as the two sides have agreed to a 21-month transition period to allow a smooth implementation of whatever Brexit deal is negotiated and minimise disruption to businesses and holidaymakers etc.

Why might Brexit take so long?

Dissolving 43 years of treaties and agreements covering thousands of different subjects was never going to be a straightforward task. It is further complicated by the fact that it has never been done before and negotiators are, to some extent, making it up as they go along. The post-Brexit trade deal is likely to be the most complex part of the negotiation because it needs the unanimous approval of more than 30 national and regional parliaments across Europe, some of whom may want to hold referendums.

So why can't the UK just cut all ties in March 2019?

The UK could cut all ties, but Theresa May and others would like to avoid such a "cliff-edge" where current regulations on things like cross-border trade and travel between the UK and the EU ends overnight. They think it would harm the economy.

What happens if there is no deal with the EU?

Without an agreement on trade, the UK would operate with the EU under World Trade Organisation rules, which could mean customs checks and tariffs on goods as well as longer border check for travellers.

There are also questions about what would happen to Britain's position as global financial centre and the land border between the UK and the Republic of Ireland. There is also concern that Brits living abroad in the EU could lose residency rights and access to free emergency health care.

What happens to EU citizens living in the UK and UK citizens in the EU?

An agreement between the UK and the EU provides what Theresa May says is certainty to the 3.2 million EU citizens in the UK - as well as citizens of Iceland, Liechtenstein, Norway and Switzerland that they will be able to carry on living and working in the UK as they have done with their rights enshrined in UK law and enforced by British courts.

UK citizens in the EU will also retain their current rights with what the EU's Jean-Claude Juncker called a cheap and simple administration procedure.

The proposal provides a cut-off date of Brexit day - 29 March 2019 - for those to be covered by the rules. Babies born after that date to people who have qualified under these rules will be included in the agreement. Under the plan EU citizens legally resident in the UK and UK citizens in the EU will be able to leave for up to five years before losing the rights they will have as part of the proposed Brexit deal.

Healthcare rights will continue as now although it is not clear yet what status an EHIC card would have for other travellers after Brexit.

How will EU citizens apply for the new status?

The full details are not yet known but UK government ministers say there will be an online system - similar to one used to renew driving licences - that will take minutes to complete with a fee similar to getting a passport, which is about £72.

Will EU nationals have to leave the UK if there is no deal?

It is not yet known what it would mean for recent arrivals. Even if no Brexit deal was done, EU nationals with a right to permanent residence, which is granted after they have lived in the UK for five years, should not see their rights affected after Brexit.

What about EU nationals who want to work in the UK?

Any EU citizen already living and working in the UK will be able to carry on working and living in the UK after Brexit. The current plan is that even after Brexit, people from the EU will be able to move to work in the UK during a "transition" phase of about two years. There is also some debate over whether they will have the same rights as those who came before, with possible restrictions on access to benefits or to vote in local elections. The EU wants them to have the same rights as now - the UK doesn't.

What happens after the transition period has yet to be decided, although it is widely expected that there will be a work permit system along the lines of that for non-EU nationals.

What does the fall in the value of the pound mean for prices in the shops?

People travelling overseas from the UK since the Brexit vote have found their pounds buy fewer euros. A slump in the value of the dollar means the exchange rate with the pound is pretty close to where it was before the referendum.

A fall in the pound means exports get a boost as UK goods will be cheaper to buy in other countries, but some imported goods could get more expensive. The latest UK inflation figures have the rate at 3%, above the target level, but not out of kilter with recent years.

Will I need a visa to travel to the EU?

The UK government wants to keep visa-free travel to the UK for EU visitors after Brexit and it is hoping this will be reciprocated, meaning UK citizens will continue to be able to visit EU countries for short periods without seeking official permission to travel.

If visitors from EU countries wanted to work, study or settle in the UK they would have to apply for permission under the proposals.

No agreement has been reached yet, however. If it is decided that EU citizens will need visas to come to the UK in the future, then UK citizens will need visas to travel to the EU.

Will I still be able to use my passport?

Yes. It is a British document - there is no such thing as an EU passport, so your passport will stay the same. The government has decided to change the colour to blue for anyone applying for a new or replacement British passport from October 2019.

Has any other member state ever left the EU?

No nation state has ever left the EU. But Greenland, one of Denmark's overseas territories, held a referendum in 1982, after gaining a greater degree of self-government, and voted by 52% to 48% to leave, which it duly did after a period of negotiation.

How will pensions, savings, investments and mortgages be affected?

State pensions are set to continue increasing by at least the level of earnings, inflation or 2.5% every year - whichever is the highest, no matter what happens in the Brexit negotiations.
There was an early post-referendum cut in interest rates, which has helped keep mortgage and other borrowing rates low. The reasonably strong performance of the UK economy, and the increase in inflation led to the Bank of England raising interest rates from 0.25% to 0.5% in November 2017 - the first increase in interest rates for 10 years. Interest rates going up generally

makes it more expensive to pay back a mortgage or loan - but should be good news for savers as they should get more interest on their money.

Will duty-free sales on Europe journeys return?

The reintroduction of duty-free sales as an "upside" or "silver lining" of Brexit. As with most Brexit consequences, whether this will happen depends on how negotiations with the EU play out - whether the "customs union" agreement between Britain and the EU is ended or continued.

Will EHIC cards still be valid?

If you are already living in another EU country on the day the UK leaves the bloc, 29 March 2019, your EHIC card - which entitles travellers to state-provided medical help for any condition or injury that requires urgent treatment, in any other country within the EU, as well as several non-EU countries - will continue to work.

After that date, for EU citizens wishing to travel to the UK or UK citizens wishing to travel to the EU, it is unclear about what will happen because no deal has yet been reached.
Will cars need new number plates?

Probably not, because there is no EU-wide law on vehicle registration or car number places, and the EU flag symbol is a voluntary identifier and not compulsory. The DVLA says there has been no discussion about what would happen to plates with the flag if the UK voted to leave.

Will leaving the EU mean we don't have to abide by the European Court of Human Rights?

The European Court of Human Rights (ECHR) in Strasbourg is not a European Union institution. It was set up by the Council of Europe, which has 47 members including Russia and Ukraine. So quitting the EU will not exempt the UK from its decisions. The Conservatives are committed to sticking with the Human Rights Act which requires UK courts to treat the ECHR as setting legal precedents for the UK during the Brexit process.

How will the European Court of Justice affect the UK after "Brexit"?

The Court of Justice of the European Union - to give it its full name - is the EU's highest legal authority. It is based in Luxembourg. It is an entirely different thing to the European Court of Human Rights (ECHR).

It is the ECHR not the ECJ that has often upset British politicians by making it harder, for example, to deport terrorist suspects. The ECJ interprets and enforces the rules of the single market, settling disputes between member countries over issues like free movement and trade. It is at the centre of pretty much everything the EU does and it having the power over UK actions has been a key issue for those arguing for the UK to leave to the EU to regain full sovereignty.

Prime Minister Theresa May has vowed that Britain will not be under the "direct" jurisdiction of the ECJ after Brexit. She has suggested that elements of relations could - where the UK signs up to specific EU agencies - still be covered by the ECJ after Brexit.

After that, there will need to be a new mechanism for settling disputes between the UK and the EU but what form that take has yet to be decided. There has been talk of an ombudsman, or some other third party, being appointed to settle disagreements. The initial stages of the Brexit deal, published on 8 December 2017, do also give limited powers to the ECJ in terms of EU citizens living in the UK for up to eight years.

Will the UK be able to re-join the EU in the future?

The UK would have to start from scratch with no rebate, and enter accession talks with the EU. Every member state would have to agree to the UK re-joining. With elections looming elsewhere in Europe, other leaders might not be generous towards any UK demands. New members are required to adopt the euro as their currency, once they meet the relevant criteria, although the UK could try to negotiate an opt-out.

Will the EU still use English?

Yes, there will still be 27 other EU states in the bloc, and others wanting to join in the future, and the common language tends to be English.

If I retire to Spain or another EU country will my healthcare costs still be covered?

At the moment, the large British expat community in Spain gets free access to Spanish GPs and their hospital treatment is paid for by the NHS. After they become permanent residents Spain pays for their hospital treatment.

In some other EU countries such as France expats of working age are expected to pay the same healthcare costs as locals but once they reach retirement age their medical bills are paid by the NHS.

The deal agreed in principle between the UK and the EU means the position will remain unchanged for British people living in the EU before the Brexit cut-off date (29 March 2019) - but it has yet to be decided what happens if you want to retire to somewhere in the EU after that date.

What will happen to pet passports?

The answer is that pet passports will, like everything else, form part of the negotiations.

The UK introduced the pet passport scheme in 2000, replacing the previous quarantine laws. It means you and your dog, cat or ferret can travel between the UK and the EU (and other participating countries) as long as it has a passport, a microchip and has been vaccinated against rabies.

Of course, until the UK actually leaves the EU, the scheme continues as normal.

Has Brexit made house prices fall?

So far, the answer is no. The average price for property has continued to increase, although the rate of annual price rise has slowed from 6.5% in 2016 to 2.7% in 2017, according to the Halifax. It said the slowdown was driven by a squeeze on real wage growth.

This debate now appears academic as US President Donald Trump is not a fan of the agreement, which means it is now seen as unlikely to be agreed - but whatever happens, when the UK quits the EU it will not be part of TTIP and will have to negotiate its own trade deal with the US.

Why has leaving the European Court of Human Rights been ignored?

The European Court of Human Rights is not an EU institution and that is why discussions about leaving it have not formed a key part of the Brexit debate.

The European Court of Justice - the ECJ - is one of the primary institutions of the European Union and administers EU law. So, while it might have a role in supervising a future trade deal, part of the goal of Brexit was to remove the UK from the ECJ's jurisdiction.

The European Court of Human Rights which, is a body set up not by the EU but by member states of the Council of Europe, a separate institution which contains countries that aren't EU members.

How will access to healthcare change for expats living in the EU?

After Brexit, there will be two possibilities.

The first and easiest would be that the negotiators come up with a reciprocal deal that keeps the current arrangements, or something a bit like them, in place.

If they don't, the situation will depend on the individual country where you live.

For residents from non-EU countries, and that will soon include the British citizens, they will have to finalise their residency status, acquire an Italian identity card and then apply for an Italian health insurance card.

If they visit the UK at the moment, access to the NHS for non-resident Brits is not straightforward unless you have a European health insurance card.

The right to treatment is based on residency, not on your tax status.

So, even if you live abroad and pay some British tax on a buy-to-let property for instance, you might find yourself getting a bill for any NHS treatment you end up getting while you are back in the UK.

What will happen to EU nationals with a British state pension?

If you are an EU national and you receive a British state pension, nothing much should change, because the state pension is dependent not on where you come from, but on how long you have paid National Insurance contributions in the UK.

So it doesn't matter where you come from, what counts is how much you have paid in terms of National Insurance contributions.

There is one condition to the above: that is that you have to have paid in for at least 10 years.

Under the current rules, if you are an EU citizen and haven't paid in for 10 years, you can point to any contributions you have made in your native country and say, "I paid in there", and that will count.

That works for EU countries and another 16 countries with which the UK has social security agreements.

Once we have left the EU, you will no longer be able to do that unless we negotiate new reciprocal agreements.
If we don't then potentially, if you have paid in fewer than 10 years' worth of National Insurance contributions, you will not get a British state pension.

Is it possible to be both an EU citizen and not an EU Citizen?

Anyone born in Northern Ireland has an absolute right to carry both passports.

An Irish passport holder can hold both.

The Irish document means you continue to enjoy the benefits of EU citizenship, and the British passport will give you full rights in the UK at the same time.

Anyone carrying a UK passport and one from another EU country will be considered as such.

All you have to do is remember to carry the Irish passport when you are joining the EU citizens-only queue at the airport in future.

Is there a get-out clause for Article 50?

On the face of it, it looks like once we have triggered Article 50 we are locked in, and that is certainly how the European

Parliament reads it.

And there is a view that if we were in this two-year process after triggering Article 50 and we wanted to get out of it, then ultimately that would be a decision for the European Court of Justice.

But the EU top brass never miss an opportunity to tell us what a big mistake they think we are making.

So, although suddenly announcing we don't want to leave after all would involve a huge loss of face, other European leaders might help it happen, whatever the legal protocol but all 28 EU members would have to agree.

Thanks to my friends at the BBC for assisting me with this whistle stop explanation on "Brexit"

Conclusion

Never forget my tips!

Always take them with you & refer to them when looking for property abroad!

Bonne chance and buona fortuna!

Stefano Lucatello

For more information :
Contact me on stefanol@kobaltlaw.co.uk
Or
Call me at Kobalt Law LLP on +44 (0) 207 739 1700

VISIT OUR WEBSITE AT:www.kobaltlaw.co.uk

©Copyright 2018

About the Author

Stefano Lucatello is one of the UK's leading international & foreign property law specialists.

He is Senior partner of Chelsea based international law firm Kobalt Law LLP, which helps and guides purchasers through the maze of pitfalls and problems, associated with international property purchases.

He qualified as an English Solicitor in 1988 and as a Gibraltar Solicitor in 1992, whilst being a partner of an international law firm, where he learnt his profession, as an offshore tax and trust lawyer.

He has specialised in this area of international and foreign property law for over 25 years, appearing as an expert and commentator, with recognised authorities, David and Carrie Grant and Martin Roberts, presenter of "Homes Under The Hammer".

Stefano gives lectures and seminars as well as making regular and frequent appearances on national & international television channels, including BBC TV, SKY, ITN, ITV, the South African "Arise TV" channel,and Turkish Tv's "TRT World"

He blogs and writes for newspapers and specialist property magazines, including "A Place in the Sun" and the "Financial Times".

Stefano travels regularly to Italy and other European countries, where he lectures on UK and foreign property investment topics.

He is also a sports agent and sports lawyer, having dealt with some of the most famous names in football and boxing over the years.

He lives in London with his partner Marilyn and has one son, Alessandro.

©

Visit Our Website at: WWW.KOBALTLAW.CO.UK

Testimonials

Martin Roberts. TV Property Expert, "Homes Under The Hammer" Presenter, Journalist & Author

"Buying abroad is a minefield for the unwary and unprepared. Take the potential problems of buying in the UK and multiply them tenfold when buying anywhere else. I've known Stefano for over 10 years, and there are few people, if any, with better knowledge of the complexities of overseas property law. If I was going to buy abroad again, I'd use him to protect me".

Rob Brown, bestselling author of "How to Build Your Reputation"

As somebody who has been 'burnt' when buying international property, this book is precisely the kind of resource that would have saved me a lot of pain and suffering This only logical solution is to absorb the practical insight in this excellent manual written by THE stand out expert in the field of international property law!

Peter Robinson
CEO
AIPP - Association of International Property Professionals

"The ever-energetic Stefano has been doing what he does best, for three 3 cycles of the international property market now. As such, few can match his insights, perspective and vigour in guiding his clients to realise their foreign property aspirations. With his client work, regular educational seminars & media appearances I frankly don't know how he had time to write this book".

Xavier Wiggins - GM Investorist UK
Owner of The Overseas Property Professional 2004-2014

"Controversial, charismatic and bursting with knowledge on this complex industry, Stefano is an industry 'guru', without question. As Owner of Kobalt Law LLP he has set the 'gold standard' in the multi-disciplinary minefield of international property law. As author of this long awaited and hugely valuable book he has managed to explain the often turgid (yet necessary) detail in an entertaining and powerful way. It might just save you a fortune. "

Stewart Andersen- International property writer, Journalist and TV presenter

"Many people dream of buying a home in another country. Turning the dream into reality can mean that you need professional help. Problems can arise from a lack of knowledge (legal and financial) and this is where Stefano Lucatello can step in. His book is a mine of information on every aspect of buying a home abroad and I can't recommend it enough. Get the help from an expert!"

Rita Bologna
Managing Director
The Good Property Guide

I have known stefano for many years now, and he has always shown great professionalism and insightfulness when it comes to all aspects of his work. For the majority, buying a property abroad can be a daunting process. However, with the help of this book, that process can be be made easier. I would reccommend this book to anyone thinking of buying property abroad.

Stefano Lucatello

Notes

Notes

Notes

Notes

Notes

Notes

Notes

Notes

Notes

Notes

Notes

Notes

Notes

Notes

Notes

Notes

Notes

Notes

Notes

Notes

Notes

Notes